LEFT-HANDED STITCHERY

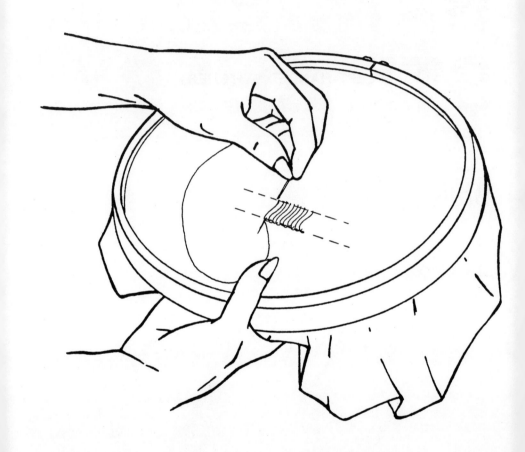

LEFT-HANDED STITCHERY

Sally Cowan

Illustrations by Kurt Loftus

4880 Lower Valley Road, Atglen, PA 19310

Dedicated to my husband, who may be right, but who encourages me to be left.

ACKNOWLEDGMENTS

In addition to Kurt Loftus's patience, (Kurt, a right-handed non-sewer endlessly redrew stitch diagrams), I enjoyed my father's expertise with the camera for the first pictures of the left-handed embroidery stitches.

I would also like to thank my friend and editor, Kathleen Hawk, for helping me make it all readable.

New material Copyright © 1987 by Sally Cowan
Library of Congress Catalog Number: 87-061438

All rights reserved. No part of this work may be reproduced or used in any form or by any means—graphic, electronic, or mechanical, including photocopying or information storage and retrieval systems—without written permission from the publisher.

The scanning, uploading and distribution of this book or any part thereof via the Internet or via any other means without the permission of the publisher is illegal and punishable by law. Please purchase only authorized editions and do not participate in or encourage the electronic piracy of copyrighted materials.

"Schiffer," "Schiffer Publishing Ltd. & Design," and the "Design of pen and inkwell" are registered trademarks of Schiffer Publishing Ltd.

ISBN: 978-0-88740-110-7
Printed in China

Schiffer Books are available at special discounts for bulk purchases for sales promotions or premiums. Special editions, including personalized covers, corporate imprints, and excerpts can be created in large quantities for special needs. For more information contact the publisher.

Published by Schiffer Publishing Ltd.
4880 Lower Valley Road
Atglen, PA 19310
Phone: (610) 593-1777; Fax: (610) 593-2002
E-mail: Info@schifferbooks.com

For the largest selection of fine reference books on this and related subjects, please visit our web site at
www.schifferbooks.com
We are always looking for people to write books on new and related subjects. If you have an idea for a book please contact us at the above address.

This book may be purchased from the publisher.
Include $5.00 for shipping.
Please try your bookstore first.
You may write for a free catalog.

In Europe, Schiffer books are distributed by
Bushwood Books
6 Marksbury Ave.
Kew Gardens
Surrey TW9 4JF England
Phone: 44 (0) 20 8392 8585; Fax: 44 (0) 20 8392 9876
E-mail: info@bushwoodbooks.co.uk
Website: www.bushwoodbooks.co.uk

CONTENTS

FOREWORD............ 4
STITCHERY BASICS....... 5

1. STRAIGHT STITCHES
   Running stitch........... 9
   Whipped running stitch.. 10
   Fern stitch.............. 10
   Seeding stitch.......... 12

2. BACKSTITCHES
   Backstitch.............. 13
   Threaded backstitch..... 14
   Pekinese stitch......... 16
   Outline stitch.......... 17
   Split stitch............. 18

3. CAUGHT STITCHES
   Fly stitch.............. 19
   Feather stitch.......... 21
   Wheatsheaf stitch....... 22
   Lattice stitch........... 24
   Open cretan stitch...... 24

4. BLANKET AND BUTTONHOLE STITCHES
   Blanket stitch........... 25
   Closed buttonhole stitch................ 26
   Buttonhole ring......... 26

5. CHAIN STITCHES
   Chain stitch............ 27
   Zigzag chain stitch...... 28
   Lazy daisy stitch........ 30
   Feather chain stitch..... 31
   Ladder stitch.......... 33
   Wheat ear stitch........ 34
   Knotted chain stitch..... 36
   Double chain stitch...... 38
   Tete de boeuf stitch..... 40
   Tete de boeuf variation stitch................ 40

6. KNOTTED STITCHES
   French knot stitch....... 41
   Bullion stitch........... 43
   Rope stitch............. 45

7. CROSS STITCH
   Cross stitch............ 46
   Herringbone stitch...... 47
   Threaded herringbone... 48
   Fishbone stitch......... 49

8. COUCHING STITCHES
   Simple couching stitch.. 50
   Satin couching stitch.... 52
   Roumanian couching stitch................ 53

9. SATIN STITCHES
   Satin stitch............. 55
   Encroaching satin stitch................ 56
   Long-and-short stitch... 56
   Padded satin stitch...... 58

10. LAID FILLING STITCHES
   Trellis stitch............ 59
   Intersected trellis stitch.. 60
   Back-and cross-stitch... 61
   Block filling stitch....... 61

FOREWORD

It has been suggested by research that we left-handed people are more creative and more persistent in temperament than the rest of the population. I might add that creativity and persistence are the perfect qualities to have when "left" behind by right-handed instructions and diagrams for sewing and needlework.

I wrote my first book, *Left-Handed Sewing,* because I felt a common bond between myself and those countless lefthanders who have tried to follow sewing diagrams by turning them upside down or by holding them up to a mirror. As a student seamstress, and later as a teacher, whether I was trying to learn from the right or teach my right-handed students from the left, I have seen and experienced the frustrations of being "wrong-handed"

Here, at last, can be an end to the confusion. *Left-handed Stitchery* is a book by a left-handed seamstress and needlewoman for left-handed sewers. All the diagrams were done for left-handers. It was written with affection and optimism, because, after all, if you had enough interest to pick up this book, you have the creativity and persistence to succeed.

In this book I have gone beyond the basic sewing skills taught in *Left-Handed Sewing* and focused on the "fancy" decorative stitches that have challenged and delighted needlewomen for centuries. Each stitch is discussed individually, and line drawings illustrate the movement of needle thread. Most stitches have many variations, created by changing the length or direction of the stitch, or by working them in combination. Once the basic stitch is mastered, others in the same family are easy to learn.

Stitchery should never leave you tied up in knots; rather, it should be an enjoyable activity that yields satisfying results. I hope that this book untangles any frustrations and difficulties you may have encountered while learning new stitches from right-handed books, and it is in that spirit that I say "Left on!"

STITCHERY BASICS

Embroidery stitches have long been known as "fancy work" because usually they serve no function other than decoration. Unlike ordinary sewing stitches, which join seams, fasten hems, reinforce buttonholes, and do all the other practical jobs of tailoring, embroidery, or "stitchery," is meant to delight the eye. It adds color, texture, and character.

The history of embroidery is undoubtedly tied to the origins of sewing. In the same way that creative techniques evolved to minimize stress on the seams of a hide garment, techniques evolved to work handsome patterns in straw, grass, or quills on smooth surfaces or edges.

The basic stitches of embroidery have changed little since medieval times, when fancy work was a cottage industry for peasants and a favorite diversion for aristocratic women. That is not to say that our medieval forebears, who worked so painstakingly by the light of candles or oil lamps (perhaps with yarns they wove and dyed themselves) would not be amazed at what modern needleworkers are doing today. We have a variety of materials and colors heretofore unheard of; we have knowledge of techniques from cultures around the world; most important, we live in a time when creativity is highly valued. The same stitches that delicately embellish an infant's christening robe can be boldly worked in heavy yarn on a wall hanging. The same bright patterns that illuminate a peasant tunic can be worked on canvas to make a hearth rug.

FABRIC

Crewel and other kinds of stitchery with freeform patterns are usually worked on common-weave fabrics. Common-weave fabrics include most woven fabrics used for clothing. They must be smoothly and tightly woven. Medium-weight fabrics, such as linen and lightweight wools, may be easier for a beginner to work, but cotton and synthetics, from sheer organdy to heavy crepe, can also be embroidered. Most knits are not suitable.

Even-weave fabrics (a refinement of common-weave fabric) has a precise number of stitches per square inch. These fabrics may be used for blackwork, huck, and other counted-thread techniques. Even-weaves may be as tightly woven as some common-weave fabrics, and are, therefore, usuable for virtually any kind of embroidery. Special even-weaves such as hardanger cloth, which has threads woven in pairs, or aida cloth, which has groups of threads woven to leave a regular grid of prick marks in the fabric, are used for counted cross stitch.

Patterned fabrics, such as checked gingham or dotted fabrics, are also popular for embroidery. The pattern supplies a visual grid for stitches such as cross stitch, feather stitch, and others. Huckaback, a 17-inch-wide toweling fabric for huck embroidery, has raised threads at regular intervals. Other woven patterns, such as striped ticking or damask, and printed patterns, such as cretonne, can provide a framework for embroidery design.

THREADS

Embroidery can be worked in virtually any kind of yarn or thread. Even raffia is used to decorate straw bags. The most important consideration is to match the weight of the thread to the fabric that is being embroidered.

Some embroidery stitches, particularly filling stitches such as satin stitch or couching stitch, use a quantity of thread in a relatively small area.

Thread that is too heavy can literally weigh down a garment. Though different kinds of embroidery stitches require specific weights of yarn, a general rule is that the thread should be no more than double the weight of the individual threads of the fabric being worked.

Some additional facts and helpful hints about threads are these:

Working lengths of yarn or thread should be no more than 18 inches to prevent knotting and fraying.

Be sure all threads and yarns are colorfast.

Many of the threads you might use, such as embroidery floss and *Persian yarn,* are loosely twisted. The strands can be separated, as you need them, into finer strands.

Embroidery floss is a loosely twisted, six-strand yarn sold in many colors. Cotton is the most common fiber, though floss is made also in silk and rayon.

Pearl cotton is a more tightly twisted, two-strand thread. It comes in three weights and has a harder, shinier finish than embroidery floss.

Matte embroidery cotton, a firmly twisted, five-ply thread, offers a softer finish. It is difficult to separate the strands, and therefore matte embroidery cotton is used for heavier fabrics.

Crewel yarn of wool and acrylic is a fine, two-ply strand.

Persian yarn is heavier than crewel. It is formed of three strands loosely twisted. Each strand is two-ply and similar in weight to crewel.

Tapestry yarn is similar in weight to Persian, but a tightly twisted four-ply.

Knitting yarn is also four-ply, but more loosely twisted. Knitting yarn may be wool or acrylic and comes in a variety of weights. Nubby, looped, or uneven yarns are usually not suitable for embroidery.

Rug Yarn is a very bulky, three-ply made of wool, acrylic, or cotton blend. Its texture may accent other materials in an embroidered piece, or it can be stitched on burlap or heavy mesh for embroidered rugs or other massive pieces.

Metallic threads come in various weights and colors. They are used for accents, very dressy garments, and special effects. Metallic threads are usually coarse-textured and therefore are not used where they will come in contact with skin or delicate lingerie.

HOOPS AND FRAMES

Most kinds of embroidery require a hoop or frame to prevent the stitches from stretching or bunching the fabric.

Hoops are actually pairs of two hoops that fit together tightly, one over the other, to hold the fabric firmly in place. Hoops are made in plastic, metal, or wood, and may be hand-held or attached to a frame. The kind with a screw attachment on the outer frame allows you to tighten the hoops after the fabric has been inserted. The spring kind does not give you that last-minute adjustment.

Scroll frames come in a number of sizes, and many can be adjusted both in height and width. The fabric is wrapped around both top and bottom rollers, which may then be tightened. There is virtually no fear of damage to the fabric on a scroll frame.

Stretcher or slat-sided frames are rectangles of mitered slats. The fabric is stretched around the framework and tacked either to the back or the sides.

NEEDLES

Besides its obvious purpose of guiding and transporting the yarn through the fabric, an embroidery needle also protects the yarn by opening a sufficiently large hole in the fabric to allow the yarn to slip through without fraying.

Crewels are used for most embroidery. They are medium-length needles with sharp points and large eyes. They are sold in sizes from 1 to 10, 1 being the smallest.

Chenilles are also sharp, but they are thicker and have larger eyes than crewels. They are sized from 13 (the largest) to 26 and are used for heavier yarns.

Tapestry needles are sized similarly to chenilles, but have blunt, rounded points. They are used for counted-thread work and mesh fabrics.

ADDITIONAL SUPPLIES

Scissors should be sharp to prevent fraying of thread ends.
A thimble will protect your left middle finger.

A FEW POINTERS

Regardless of whether you are left-handed or right-handed, the following hints help ensure good work:

Neatness counts in embroidery on the back as well as on the side that shows. Practicing a stitch on a piece of scrap fabric will not only help you find the perfect, uniform tension, but will also teach you how to keep your work even and untangled on both sides of the fabric.

Never knot your thread or yarn. The knot may cause a bump that will show through on a garment or a framed piece. Instead, leave 2 inches of thread and stitch over it on the back of the work. Or slip the needle under a couple of inches of worked stitches to hold the yarn down. To tie off, simply reverse the process and guide the thread under the previous few inches of stitches on the back.

Do not trail thread on the back over a long expanse of fabric in order to pick up the same color in another part of the design. Trailing threads too often show through on the front of the work. Better to tie off and begin anew.

Follow the lines of a pattern printed on the fabric precisely. Frequently these lines do not wash out. If you have not covered them with thread, you may have to look at them forever.

To untwist a tangled thread, simply let the needle dangle freely. The yarn will unwind by itself.

A stabbing motion, perpendicular to the fabric, will help you find the best tension for the stitches.

1. STRAIGHT STITCHES

These are the most straightforward embroidery stitches. You simply bring the needle out then in, to leave a line of thread on the surface of the fabric. Perfect results require a uniform stitch length, so these stitches are often worked on even-weave fabric on which the fabric threads can be counted.

RUNNING STITCH

A series of straight stitches, much like basting, running stitches can be used for light outlining or as a base for other, more complex stitches. It can also be worked in rows for a light filling of color. Usually this stitch is worked with more thread showing on the front of the fabric than on the back. As few as one or two threads of the fabric may be picked up between stitches.

Start on the left. Bring the needle through to the front of the fabric and then take several stitches of equal length before pulling the needle through the fabric (Figs. 1—1A and B).

Running stitch

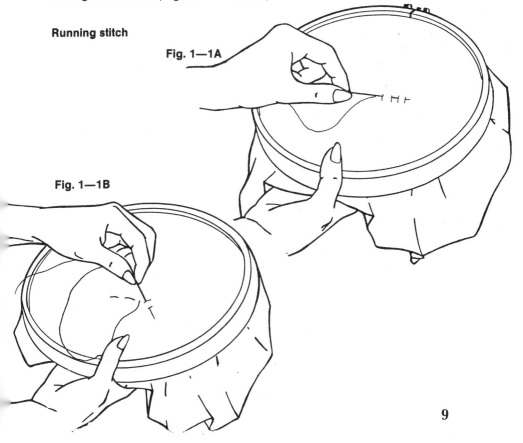

Fig. 1—1A

Fig. 1—1B

WHIPPED RUNNING STITCHES

For a heavier, raised outline or a two-color effect, the running stitch can be "whipped" with a second thread. First work a row of running stitches (Fig. 1—1A). Then, with another thread of the same or a different color, bring the needle through to the front of the fabric at the center of the first stitch on the left. Without piercing the fabric or the running stitches, slide the needle under the next stitch from left to right. Repeat down the row of stitches (Fig. 1—2). If it is too difficult to avoid pricking the material or splitting the stitches, try slipping the eye of the needle, rather than its point, under each stitch.

Whipped running stitch

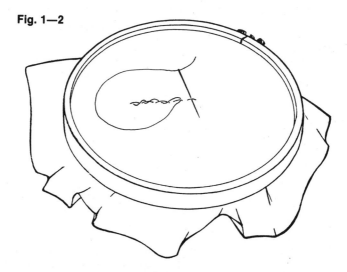

Fig. 1—2

FERN STITCH

This graceful stitch, which looks like a spray of tiny leaves, is only a series of straight stitches in a regular pattern.

Working from left to right, bring the needle through to the front of the fabric at the base of the stem. Insert the point of the needle through the fabric a stitch-length away on the stem and bring it to the front again at an angle forward and to the right (Fig. 1—3A). Pull the needle through. Insert the needle at the top of the stem stitch and bring it to the front again at an angle to the left (B). Pull the needle through. Beginning at the top of the stem, begin the pattern again (C and D). Be careful not to pull the thread too tightly.

Fern stitch

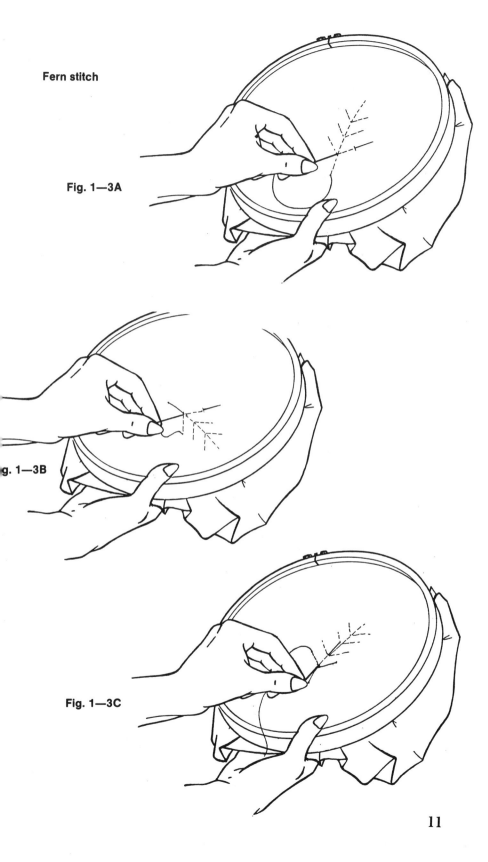

Fig. 1—3A

Fig. 1—3B

Fig. 1—3C

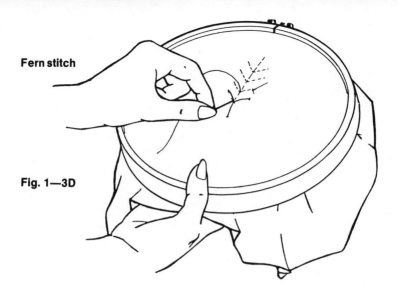

Fern stitch

Fig. 1—3D

SEEDING STITCH

The seeding stitch is a detached filling stitch that can be worked long or short, in clusters or scattered, close together or far apart. Most frequently seeding is arranged to appear random, by working the stitches in many directions, but the stitches can also be patterned for a uniform appearance. Seeding is most effective in darker colors, because light thread may not show up on the fabric.

Begin to work a backstitch into the fabric, but bring the needle through to the front in the same hole just made by the needle for one thread instead of ⅛-inch to the right. Repeat, using the same holes at each end. The two stitches should lay neatly side by side. Even in random placement, spaces between the stitches should be uniform for a balanced appearance. (See Fig. 1—4).

Seeding stitch

Fig. 1—4

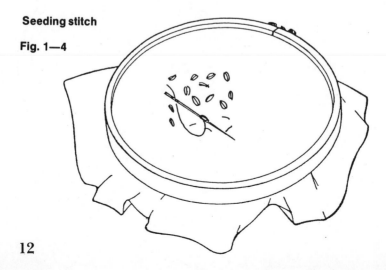

2. BACKSTITCHES

This family of stitches, characterized by a stitching motion of one step backwards and two steps ahead, is commonly used for outlines, straight and curved lines, and for foundation outlines under the satin stitch.

BACKSTITCH

This stitch produces a neat line and is especially good for straight outlines. If a curved line is needed, the stitches must be worked very small.

Work from left to right. For a stitch ¼-inch long, bring the needle through to the front of the fabric ⅛-inch to the right of the beginning of the line. Insert the needle at the beginning of the line ⅛-inch to the left and bring it back up to the front ¼-inch to the right (Fig. 2—1A). Continue with the following sequence: Insert the needle ⅛-inch to the left (at the right end of the previous completed stitch) and bring it through to the front of the fabric ¼-inch to the left (B). Keep the stitches firm and even.

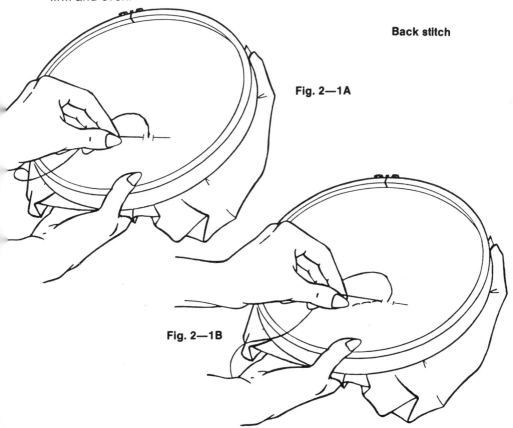

Back stitch

Fig. 2—1A

Fig. 2—1B

THREADED BACKSTITCH

The backstitch may be "whipped" or threaded (using the technique shown for the whipped running stitch) for another decorative border or outline effect. As in the whipped stitch, different colors may be used for the base stitch and the threading.

Work a base row of backstitches rather large (Fig. 2—2A). With a new length of thread, bring the needle to the front of the fabric at the center of the first stitch at the left. Working from left to right, slide the needle up under the thread of one stitch and down under the thread of the next (B and C). Do not pierce the fabric. Pull the thread loosely through after each stitch (D). The width of the loop is determined by the tension of the thread. Backstitches may also be double-threaded working the same technique first threading from left to right and then from right to left to create a more intricately braided effect.

Threaded backstitch

Fig. 2—2A

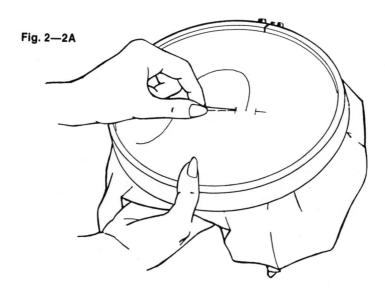

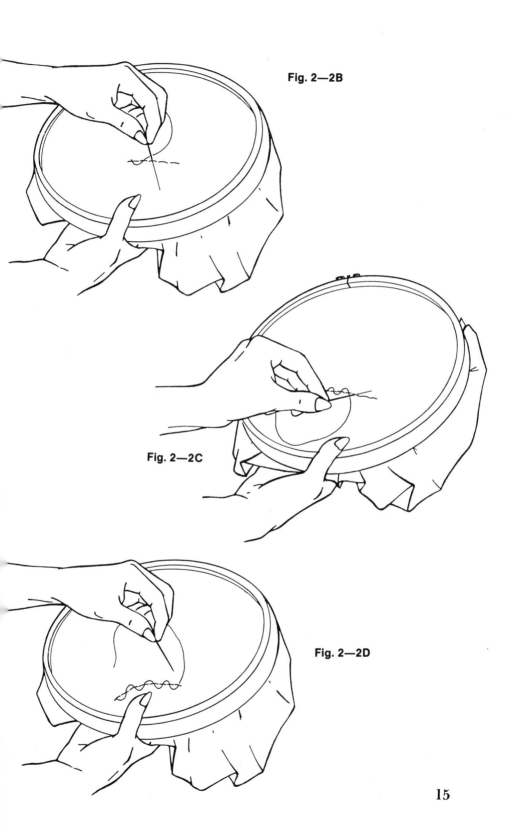

Fig. 2—2B

Fig. 2—2C

Fig. 2—2D

PEKINESE STITCH

Also known as the Chinese stitch because of its frequent use in oriental handwork, the Pekinese stitch is a variation of the threaded backstitch. The stitch may be left a little loopy or worked firmly for a braided effect. It is a pretty way to use metallic threads.

Lay a row of backstitches (Fig. 2—3A). With a new length of thread, bring the needle through to the front of the fabric at the center of the second stitch on the left. Without piercing the fabric, slide the needle down under the thread of the first backstitch and up under the thread of the third backstitch (B). Pull the needle through. Slide the needle down through the second stitch and up through the fourth stitch. Pull through and continue to the end of the line (C).

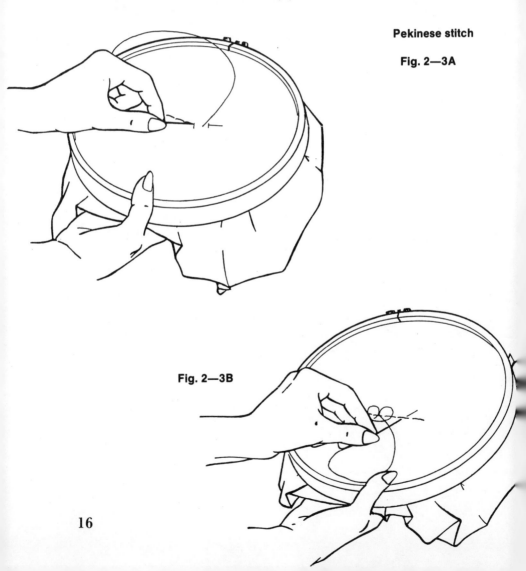

Pekinese stitch

Fig. 2—3A

Fig. 2—3B

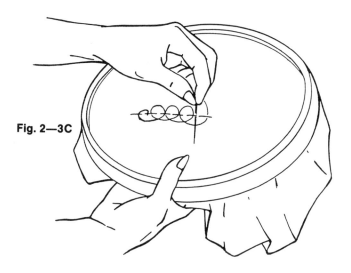

Fig. 2—3C

OUTLINE STITCH

This heavier outlining stitch produces a twisted effect. It is also known as the stem stitch or crewel stitch. In addition to working lines and outlines, this stitch can be worked in close rows for a dense filling with a woven appearance.

If you are working a curved line, be sure that the pattern is turned so that the line curves toward you. Bring the needle through to the front of the fabric at the right end of the line. Insert the needle one stitch-length to the left and back through half a stitch length, keeping the thread below the needle. Continue by inserting the needle down the line the length of a stitch and bringing it to the front of the fabric again halfway back (Fig. 2—4). Keep the stitches firm, but not so tight that the fabric pulls.

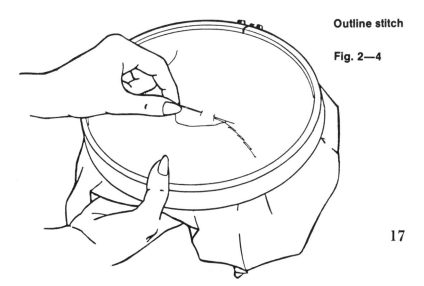

Outline stitch

Fig. 2—4

SPLIT STITCH

This stitch is worked much like the outline stitch, except that rather than lying beside it, each stitch literally splits the one before it. The split stitch requires soft thread or yarn and resembles a slender chain stitch when finished. It does well on tight curves as an outlining stitch. Worked in rows, especially with shaded thread, it is also a popular filling stitch.

Bring the needle through to the front of the fabric a half-stitch to the right of the left end of the line to be worked. Insert the needle at the beginning of the line and bring it through to the front again a full stitch-length to the right (Fig. 2—5A). Insert the needle near the top of the last stitch on the left, splitting the thread, and bring the needle through to the front of the fabric again a stitch-length to the right (B). Continue working left to right, splitting each previous stitch.

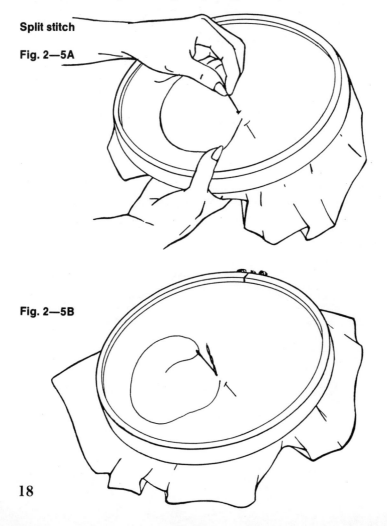

Split stitch

Fig. 2—5A

Fig. 2—5B

3. CAUGHT STITCHES

A variety of embroidery stitches owe their interesting curves to the linking of one stitch to another, which pulls the thread away from its normally straight course.

FLY STITCH

Also known as the Y-stitch, this is a kind of detached feather stitch usually used as a light filling (Fig. 3—1A). The stitches can also be worked in a row to make a border, or in adjoining rows to make a diamond-pattern filling. The tacking stitch may be short under the "wings" or longer to create the Y form.

Turn the fabric so the wings of the fly stitch will open toward the top of the frame. Bring the needle through to the front of the fabric on the right-hand side of the stitch and pull the needle through. Insert the needle to the left and bring it to the front of the fabric again at the base of the wings (B), catching the loop of thread before pulling through. Insert the needle again to complete a long or short tacking stitch (C).

Fly stitch

Fig. 3—1A

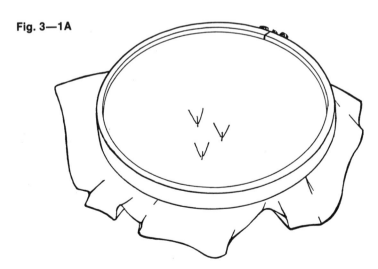

Fly stitch

Fig. 3—1B

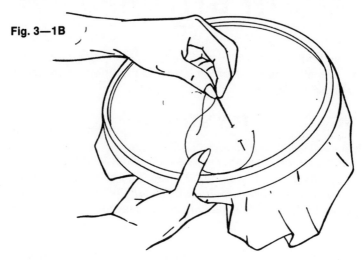

Fig. 3—1C

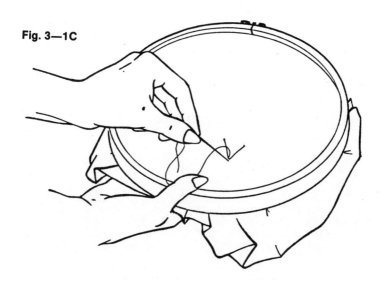

FEATHER STITCH

Also known as the coral stitch, the feather stitch is easy yet highly decorative. The airy, open stitches have been a favorite for centuries for such diverse uses as smocking, outlining crazy-quilt patches and decorating infants clothes, as well as for lacy outlines in leaf and floral designs.

Because this stitch is worked in a zigzag rhythm, it is easier to follow a double guideline. Work from top to bottom. Bring the needle through to the front of the fabric at the top of the guideline farthest from you. Insert the needle at the same height a little to the other side of the closer guideline, and bring it through to the front, down again lower on the near guideline. Pull the needle through, holding the thread lightly with your right thumb to keep it under the needle. Insert needle a little to the other side of the far guideline, and bring it to the front again lower down on the far guideline (Fig. 3—2A). Pull through, again keeping the thread below the needle. Continue in this pattern, alternating between the two guidelines (B). Take care that the stitches are of even size and tension; do not pull them too tightly.

Basic feather stitch

Fig. 3—2A

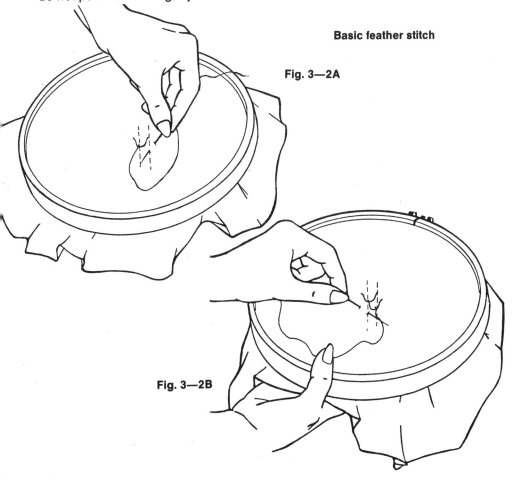

Fig. 3—2B

WHEATSHEAF STITCH

Though not strictly a loop stitch, the wheatsheaf too depends on a catching stitch to create its unique form. Also called the bundle, this filling stitch adds a strong element of color and design wherever it is used.

Working from left to right, make three long, parallel straight stitches (Figs. 3—3A) and (B). After the last stitch, bring the needle to the front of the fabric in the middle of the center stitch and slide it out to the right without pricking the threads. Without entering the fabric again, make two overcast stitches around the sheaf (C) and then insert the needle through to the back of the fabric at the same point under the bundle (D). Pull the thread through tightly enough to bind the sheaf.

Wheatsheaf stitch

Fig. 3—3A

Fig. 3—3B

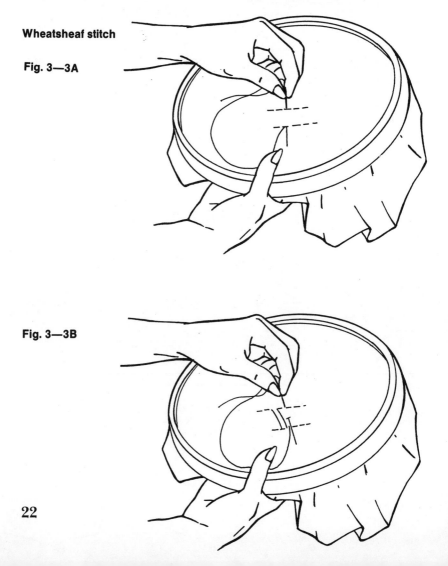

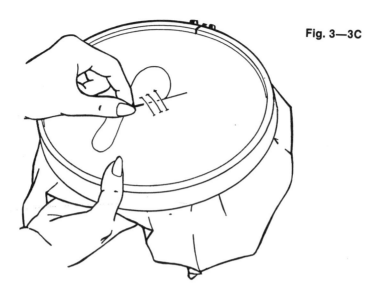

Fig. 3—3C

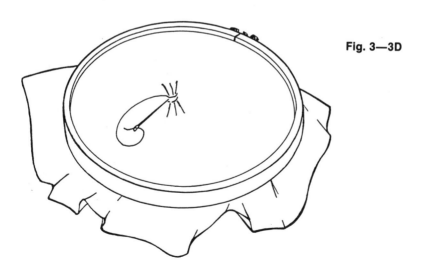

Fig. 3—3D

LATTICE STITCH

A variation on the single feather, the lattice stitch makes an airy border that is particularly effective worked small on baby clothes or lingerie. To make this stitch, simply work feather stitches on either side of a pattern line. (Fig. 3—4). Beginning at the left, bring the needle through to the front of the fabric just below the pattern line. Insert the needle far on the other side of the pattern line but even with the spot the thread emerged. Bring the needle through to the front again on the same side of the line, but closer to the line and down to the right, holding the thread lightly with your right thumb to keep it under the needle. Insert the needle far on the other side of the pattern line, and bring the needle to the front again on the same side of the line, a little to the right again keeping the thread under the needle. Finish by tacking down the last feather.

Lattice stitch

Fig. 3—4

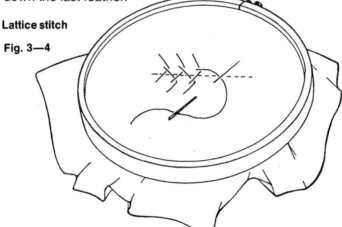

OPEN CRETAN STITCH

A filling stitch popular for leaf shapes, the open cretan stitch is worked exactly like the lattice stitch. The only difference is that the size of the stitch is gauged to the outer dimensions of the shape to be filled (Fig. 3—5).

Open cretan stitch

Fig. 3—5

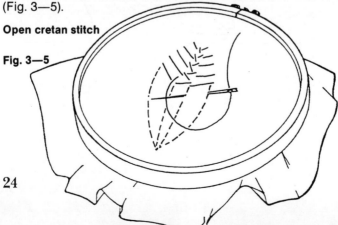

4. BLANKET AND BUTTON-HOLE STITCHES

These stitches are close relations of the feather stitch, but produce a very different effect. Both kinds of stitches are used for edging and binding in tailoring and, as might be expected, they are used primarily for the same purposes in embroidery.

BLANKET STITCH

Also known as the open buttonhole stitch, this stitch was named for its usefulness in finishing the rough edges of woolen blankets. As an embroidery stitch, blanket stitch is frequently used to finish turned raw edges. It also serves as an outlining stitch or, in joined rows, as a filling stitch with a brick-like appearance.

Turn the fabric so that the edge or line to be worked runs from left to right. Mark the fabric with one line to show the upper extension of the stitches and another line to show the baseline (unless the baseline is the edge of the fabric). Beginning on the right, bring the needle through to the front of the fabric at the end of the baseline, holding down the thread with your right thumb while you insert the needle into top guideline a little to the left and bring it through to the front again directly below on the baseline, or under the edge of the fabric. (In binding a raw edge, the needle will enter the fabric only on the top guideline.) Pull through, making sure the needle is over the loop of thread and catches it (Fig. 4—1). Continue working to the left.

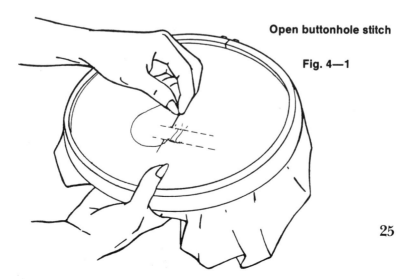

Open buttonhole stitch

Fig. 4—1

CLOSED BUTTONHOLE STITCH

This strong stitch is used to secure the edges in cutwork and open work. A line of running stitches is usually worked first to hold and mark the edge. The closed buttonhole stitch is then worked over the running stitches.

The closed buttonhole stitch is worked exactly the same as the blanket stitch, except that stitches are placed very close together to make a solid edge (Fig. 4—2).

Closed buttonhole stitch

Fig. 4—2

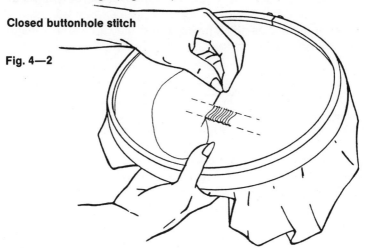

BUTTONHOLE RING

This fancy stitch for floral motifs can be worked with widely spaced stitches or closely packed ones. The illustration shows a ring worked from the circumference of a circle into the center point. An open variation can be worked on two concentric circles, with the "legs" of the buttonhole ending on the inside circle.

Work the buttonhole stitch in a clockwise direction, using the circumference as the guideline for the stitches (Fig. 4—3). Insert the needle at the same point at the center of the circle for each stitch.

Buttonhole ring

Fig. 4—3

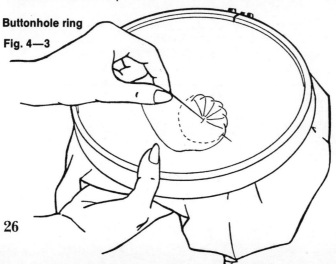

5. CHAIN STITCHES

Chain stitches are caught stitches with their loops completed where they began, creating complete links to be tacked down by the subsequent stitches.

CHAIN STITCH

One of the most popular stitches in handwork, the chain forms a broad outlining stitch or, used in rows following the outline of a motif, gives a dense, textured filling.

Turn fabric so that the guideline runs from top to bottom. Bring the needle through to the front of the fabric at the top of the guideline. Holding the base of the thread down with the right thumb, insert needle through to the back of the fabric at the same point where the thread emerged. Bring the needle to the front again a stitch-length down the guideline, keeping the thread loop under the needle (Figs. 5—1A and B). Continue in the same fashion. Tack down the last loop with a short stitch.

If used as a filling stitch, the chain stitch should always be worked in the same direction. Begin with the outer boundaries of the motif and work inward with parallel rows. If necessary, finish the small inner spaces with partial rows.

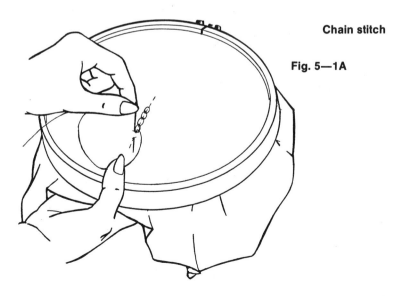

Chain stitch

Fig. 5—1A

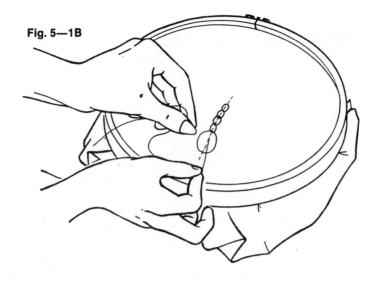

Fig. 5—1B

ZIGZAG CHAIN STITCH

This variation is used for borders and lines. Mark the fabric with two parallel lines. Work exactly as for the chain stitch, but begin on the guideline to the right and bring the needle to the front again (to tack down the loop and begin the next loop) on the opposite guideline, a short way down the pattern (Fig. 5—2A). After the first stitch, pierce the previous loop of thread when completing the link (B and C). This step ensures that the stitches lie flat.

Zigzag stitch

Fig. 5—2A

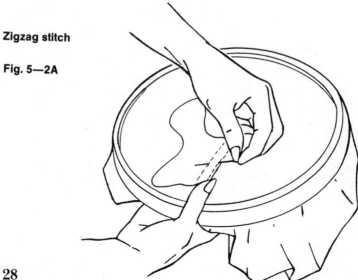

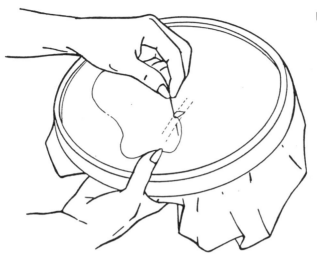

Fig. 5—2B

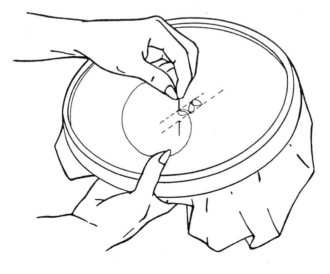

Fig. 5—2C

LAZY DAISY STITCH

This is actually a detached chain stitch worked in a circular pattern. Individual daisy stitches are also pretty as tiny leaves or scattered, like fly stitches, for a light filling.

This stitch is worked from the center of the "petals" to the outer rim of the pattern. Bring the needle through to the front of the fabric in the center of the flower and insert the needle again at the same point, holding down the thread with your right thumb. Bring the needle through to the front again at the far edge of the petal (Fig. 5—3A). Keeping the loop of thread under the needle, pull through and adjust the loop. Insert the needle again where it just emerged to form a tack over the loop (B). Bring the needle to the front of the fabric again at the inner side of the next petal. Turn the fabric as you work clockwise.

Lazy daisy stitch

Fig. 5—3A

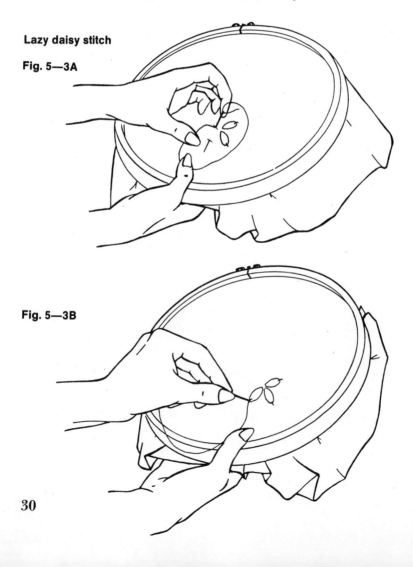

Fig. 5—3B

FEATHER CHAIN STITCH

This is a formal but delicate border stitch. It is not an easy stitch to keep even. Therefore, it requires at least the double guidelines shown in Fig. 5—4, and it is probably better worked on open-weave fabric on which the threads can be counted.

Working from top to bottom, bring the needle through to the front of the fabric at the top of one of the lines. Securing the base of the thread with your right thumb, insert the needle again at the same place and bring it to the front again on the diagonal, down and one-third of the way across the space between the guidelines (Fig. 5—4A). Keeping the loop of thread under the needle, pull the needle through. Continuing on the same angle from the first stitch, insert the needle another third of the way across the space and turn it to bring it out to the front of the fabric on the other guideline, at the same level as the end of the last loop (B). Pull the needle through. Insert the needle again at the same point where it just emerged, and bring it to the front again at the base of the last diagonal crossbar (C) to catch the chain. Continue in this fashion, keeping the angle of the slant the same on each side (D).

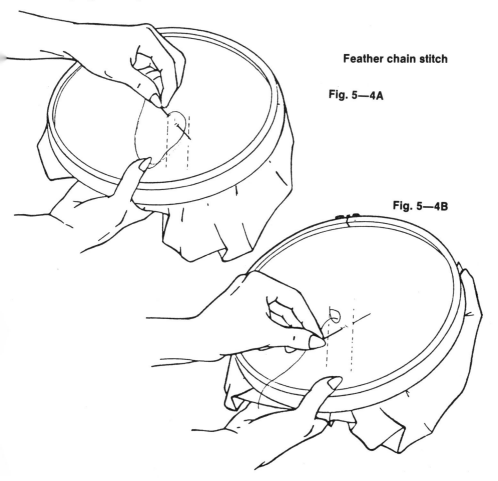

Feather chain stitch

Fig. 5—4A

Fig. 5—4B

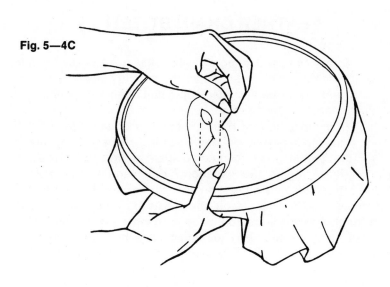

Fig. 5—4C

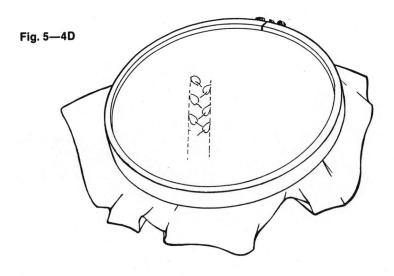

Fig. 5—4D

LADDER STITCH

Also known as the square chain stitch, this stitch creates a broad line or border. It can also be used as "beading" through which a ribbon can be threaded.

Draw parallel guidelines on the fabric and work the stitch from top to bottom. Bring the thread through to the front of the fabric on the top of the right guideline. Insert the needle at the top of the left guideline and bring it to the front of the fabric again a stitch-length down the right guideline (Fig. 5—5A). Pull through over the loop of thread, leaving some slack in the loop for later adjustment. On the left line, insert the needle through the loop opposite the point where it just emerged on the right guideline. Bring the needle to the front again on the right guideline, a stitch-length down the line (B). Pull through, keeping the needle over the new loop of thread. Adjust the tension of the first stitch and continue in this fashion.

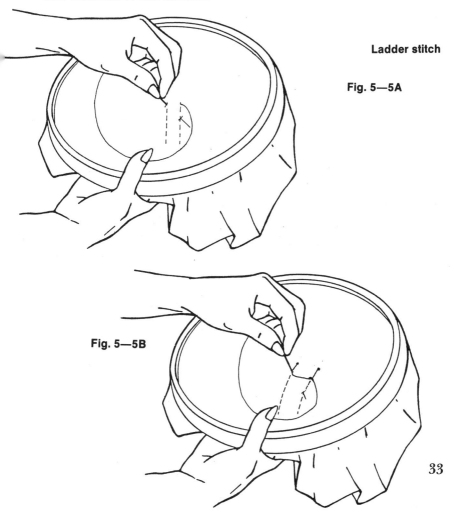

Ladder stitch

Fig. 5—5A

Fig. 5—5B

WHEATEAR STITCH

As its name suggests, this stitch is perfect for embroidering spikes of wheat in a needlework pattern as well as being a decorative border stitch.

Work from top to bottom along a guideline. Bring the needle through to the front of the fabric to the left of the guideline. Insert it on the guideline, a little lower, and bring it to the front again on the right of the guideline, opposite to where the thread first emerged. (Fig. 5—6A). Pull the needle through. Insert the needle into the same point on the guideline, finishing the wings of the stitch, and bring the needle to the front of the fabric a stitch-length down the guideline (B). Now slide the needle from left to right under the two stitches of the wings and pull the thread through gently. Insert the needle into the same point where the thread emerged (C). Bring the needle through to the front again on the right side of the guideline, a little higher up than the point at which it was inserted. Pull the needle through gently. Now you are ready to begin the next set of wings. On subsequent stitches, slip the loop thread under the base of the previous loop as well as under the wings (D).

Wheatear stitch

Fig. 5—6A

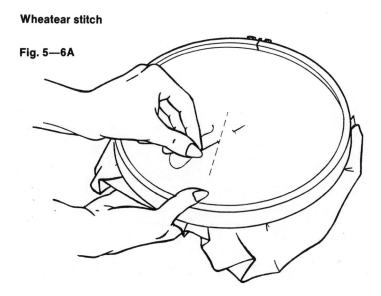

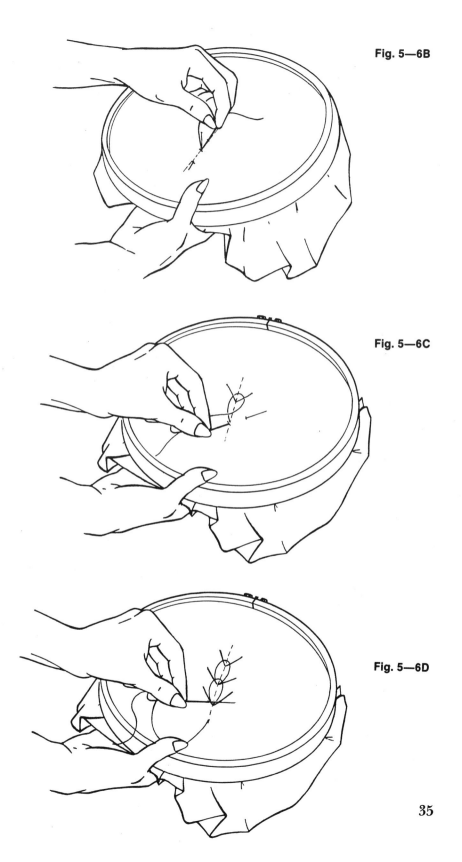

Fig. 5—6B

Fig. 5—6C

Fig. 5—6D

KNOTTED CHAIN STITCH

This stitch is easy to work, but makes an elegant border, especially with a heavier or corded thread. It can be worked in straight or curved lines.

Work from the bottom, bringing the thread up through the fabric at the pattern line. Insert the needle into the cloth a little higher and to the left, and bring the thread out again on the other side of the line. Pull through. Let thread lie in a loose loop above the work, and pass the needle from left to right under the long stitch and over the looped thread. Pull through gently, leaving some slack in the stitch, then loop the thread again over the needle and under the point (Fig. 5—7A). Adjust the size of the loop as you pull the needle through. Begin the next stitch with another straight stitch as shown in B. Finish with a long tack stitch.

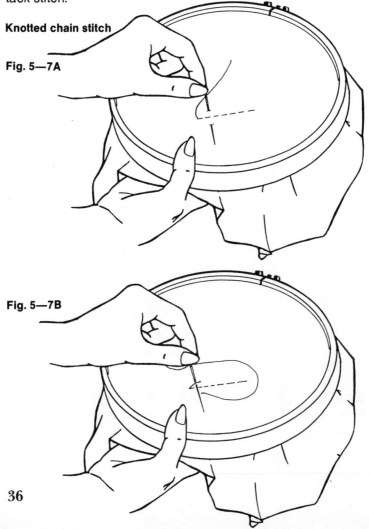

Knotted chain stitch

Fig. 5—7A

Fig. 5—7B

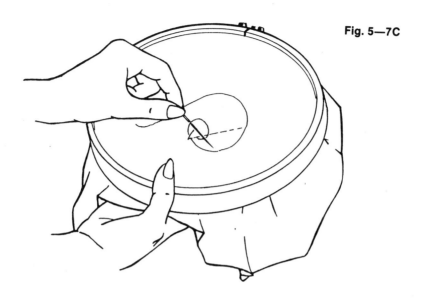

Fig. 5—7C

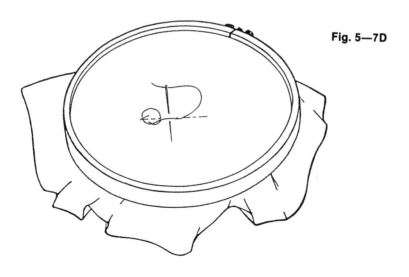

Fig. 5—7D

37

DOUBLE CHAIN STITCH

Broader and more formal-looking than the single chain stitch, the double chain stitch can also be used as a filling stitch. With the addition of a seeding stitch or french knot in the center of every loop, the stitch gains texture and depth and is appropriate for a design element such as a tree trunk.

Starting from the left, work one chain stitch (Fig. 5—8A). Loop the thread down from the chain stitch and work another partial chain (B). Work another chain out of the loop of this last stitch (C), then work another partial chain beside the first stitch (D). End with a tacking stitch over the last partial chain worked (E).

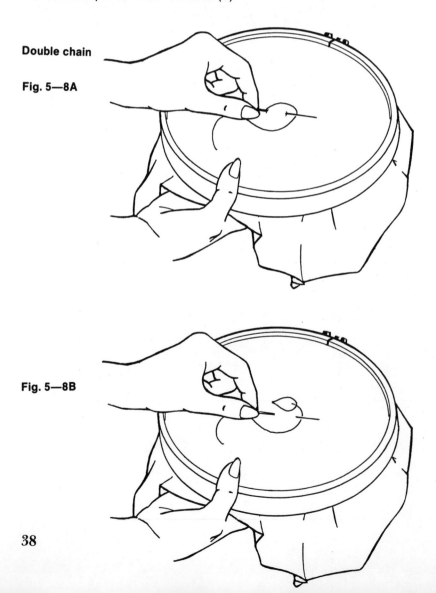

Double chain

Fig. 5—8A

Fig. 5—8B

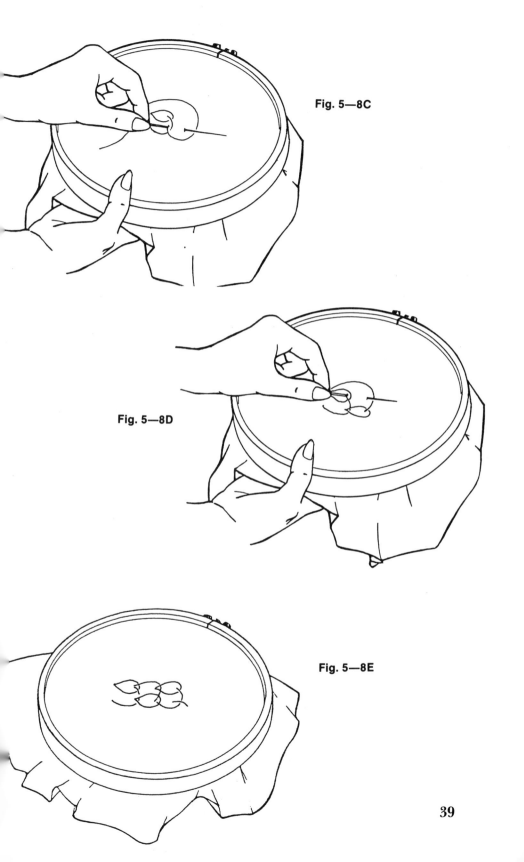

Fig. 5—8C

Fig. 5—8D

Fig. 5—8E

TETE DE BOEUF STITCH

Literally the "ox head" stitch, the tete de boeuf is a simple, overlapped variant of the lazy daisy. It is a versatile stitch, often used alone or in random groups when a bit of informal filling is needed. Arranged at the spikes of a feather stitches, the tetes look like tiny flowers. (See Fig. 5—9)

Bring the needle through to the front of the fabric, pulling the thread through. Insert the needle a short distance away, and bring it back to the front again below and between these two points. Pull the thread gently through, leaving enough slack to allow the loop to twist and creating overlapped "horns". Finish with a small tacking stitch.

Tete de boeuf stitch

Fig. 5—9

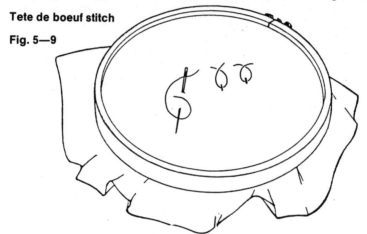

TETE DE BOEUF VARIATION STITCH

This tete de boeuf variation is a graceful and rather formal filling stitch. Worked in alternating positions on parallel rows, this variation is made of lazy daisy chains, with two straight stitches worked in a chevron formation beneath them. (See Fig. 5—10)

Tete de Boeuf variation

Fig. 5—10

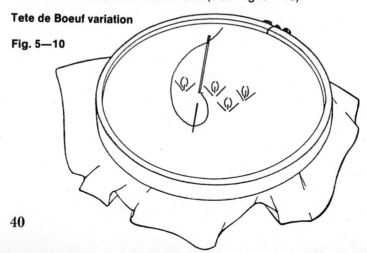

6. KNOTTED STITCHES

Knots are created by winding the thread several times around the needle before it is pulled through to the back of the fabric. Knots are all a little tricky and require some practice. While they are often used for scattered filling stitches, their shapes also make them very useful for certain designs that require a raised, well defined element. Take care not to catch finished knots under the hoop; they can easily be damaged.

FRENCH KNOT STITCH

A popular stitch, the French knot makes a single raised dot. It is used as a filling stitch, as well as clustered for the center of flowers or tiny sheep or trees. It can also be an elegant tacking stitch for stitches like the fly stitch or the lazy daisy.

Bring the thread through the fabric at the point where the knot will be positioned. On the front of the fabric, hold the thread taut with the right hand. Twist the thread two or three times around the needle (Fig. 6—1A) and pull the thread to tighten it (B). Turn the needle back and insert it again close to where the thread emerged from the cloth (C). Continuing to hold the thread taut, pull the needle through to the back of the fabric. The result will be a tiny knot lying on the surface of the fabric (D).

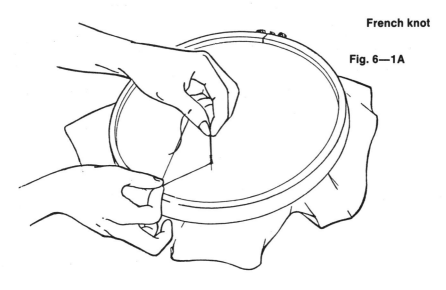

French knot

Fig. 6—1A

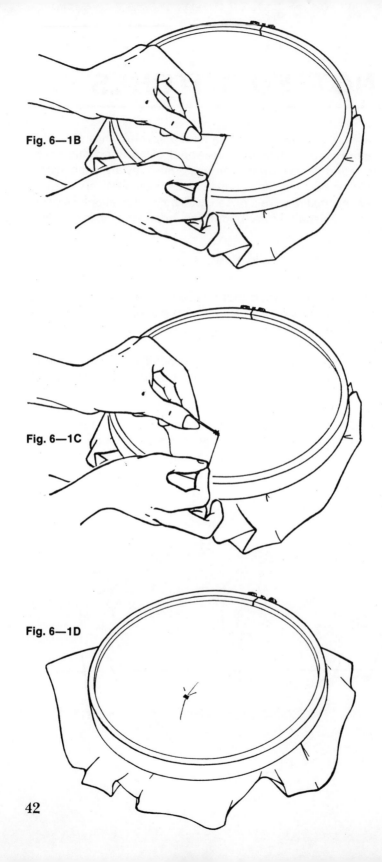

Fig. 6—1B

Fig. 6—1C

Fig. 6—1D

BULLION STITCH

Known by many other names (including the caterpillar stitch and the coil stitch), the bullion stitch looks like a short length of thickly twisted rope. It is useful for heavy outlining, for tiny flower petals, and for rosebuds; and, when worked in a dense coil, it is known as a Porto Rico rose.

Bring the needle through to the front of the fabric at the right end of the area to be covered (2). Insert it at the left end (1) and bring the point up again at the original place (2) on the right (Fig. 6—2A). Do not pull the needle through the fabric. Using your right hand, twist the thread around the end of the needle. Six or seven twists is usual, but the number depends on the distance to be covered (B). Place your right thumb on the coil and carefully pull the needle through. Once the needle is free of the coil, pull the needle and thread to the left, forcing the coil to lie flat on the fabric (C). Take the needle to the back of the fabric by inserting at point 1 on the left (D). Pull the needle through, leaving a coil of thread around the stitch (E). A curved stitch can be made by adding more twists to the needle. This stitch requires some practice and is more easily worked with a heavier thread or yarn.

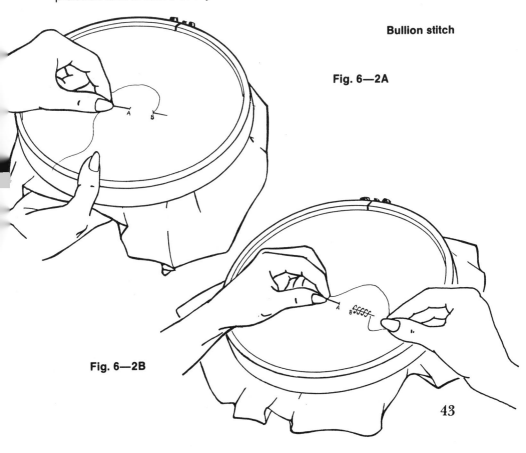

Bullion stitch

Fig. 6—2A

Fig. 6—2B

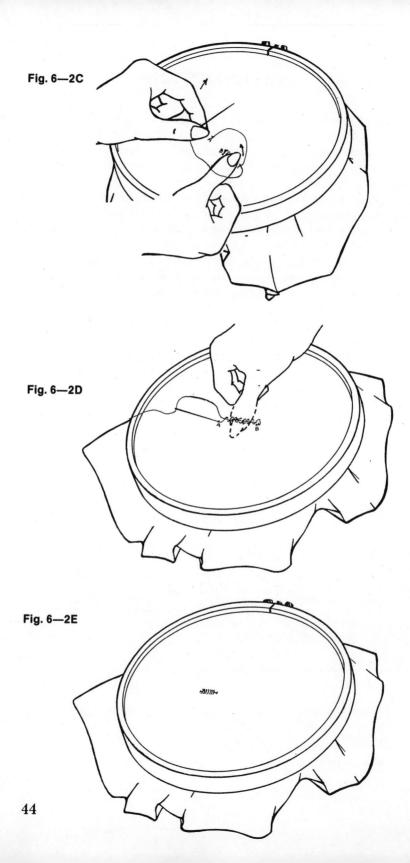

Fig. 6—2C

Fig. 6—2D

Fig. 6—2E

ROPE STITCH

The effect of this stitch is like that of a row of slanting satin stitches, except that hidden knots give height on the lower edge. The rope stitch is best used on a curved line and produces effective wide borders and stems.

Working from left to right, bring the needle through to the front of the fabric on the end of the lower guideline. Insert the needle farther back to the left at a slant, along the upper guideline, and bring it to the front again on the lower guideline very close to where it first emerged. Using your right hand, slip the thread under the needle and pull the needle through (Fig. 6—3). Continue, keeping the stitches closely placed to hide the little knots. Finish by tacking down the last loop.

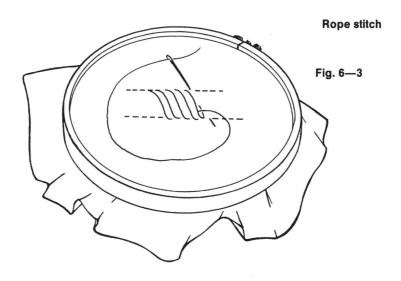

Rope stitch

Fig. 6—3

7. CROSS STITCHES

One of the best-known stitches in handwork, the cross stitch is the base of a whole family of stitches formed by two straight stitches that cross each other, usually on the diagonal.

CROSS STITCH

This is a fast and easy stitch that requires only evenness in size to be an effective filling stitch, border stitch, or outline stitch. It is flexible enough to be the base for intricate floral patterns and letter forms.

Cross stitch, unlike its variations, can be worked most quickly and evenly in two journeys across the fabric. The stitch should be worked either as counted-thread work on open-weave fabric or with printed guidelines on common-weave to ensure regular size and shape. Working first from left to right, bring the needle through to the front of the fabric at the lower left point of the first stitch. Insert the needle at the upper right point and bring the needle through to the front of the fabric again at the lower left point of the next stitch. Pull the needle through and continue to the end of the row (Fig. 7—1A). To return, bring the needle through to the front of the fabric at the lower right point of the last stitch on the left. Insert the needle into the upper left point and bring it through to the front again at the lower left point of the next stitch (B). This produces a stitch with the upper diagonal running from lower right to upper left. Make sure all stitches on the piece have the upper stitch running the same way.

Cross stitch

Fig. 7—1A

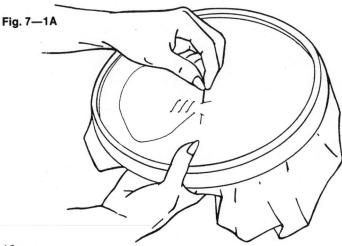

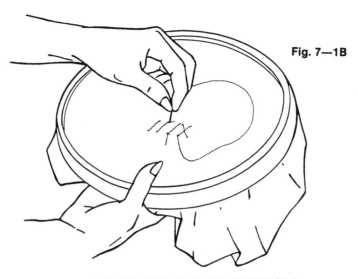

Fig. 7—1B

HERRINGBONE STITCH

Similar to the catch stitch in weaving, the herringbone stitch is an attractive border stitch that lends itself especially well to embellishments with a second thread color. Like the cross stitch, it requires detailed guidelines or counted threads.

Working from right to left, bring the thread through to the front of the fabric at the base of the lower guideline. Insert it one stitch-length to the left on the top guideline, and bring the needle through to the front again one-third of the way back to the right on the top guideline (Fig. 7—2A). Pull the needle through. Continue, alternating the stitches on the top and bottom lines, keeping the angle of the crossing thread the same in each direction (B).

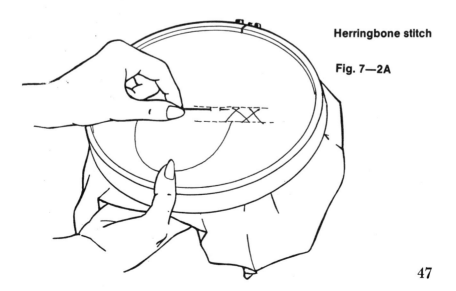

Herringbone stitch

Fig. 7—2A

Fig. 7—2B

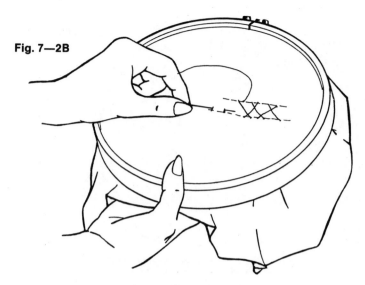

THREADED HERRINGBONE

The herringbone can be combined with other stitches to make colorful borders. One method is to tack down the stitch-crossings with contrasting thread. Another, the threaded herringbone, weaves the second color through the stitches.

Work a line of herringbone and end off the first color. With a new length of thread, bring the needle through to the front of the fabric at the far end of the first stitch on the right. Wrap the thread around the leg of the stitch without piercing the fabric. Then slide the needle under the next leg to the left, wrapping the leg in the opposite direction (Fig. 7—3A). Continue wrapping in alternating directions, adjusting the second thread to cover the crossings in the first stitches (B).

Threaded herringbone stitch

Fig. 7—3A

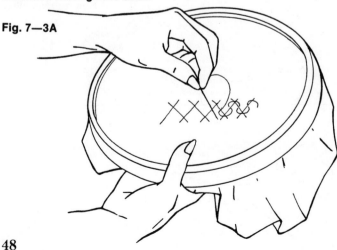

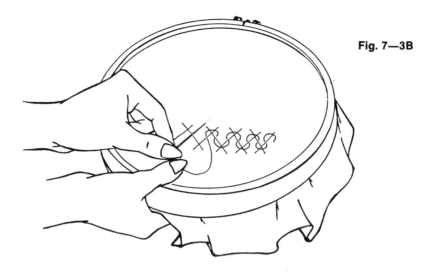

Fig. 7—3B

FISHBONE STITCH

This fishbone stitch is closely related to cross stitch, but provides a solid filling of color with a raised central rib. It is frequently used for leaf designs.

For a leaf or lozenge shape, begin with a short straight stitch at the top point of the shape. Bring the needle through to the front of the fabric at the top of the right outline of the design, immediately beside the straight stitch. Insert it a little to the left of the center line, a little below the straight stitch. Bring the needle through to the front again on the top of the left boundary of the shape. Pull the needle through. Continue this pattern on alternate sides, keeping the stitches close together for a solid filling. The stitches will cross slightly over the center line (Fig. 7—4). The stitches may be more widely spaced for a more open look.

Fish bone stitch

Fig. 7—4

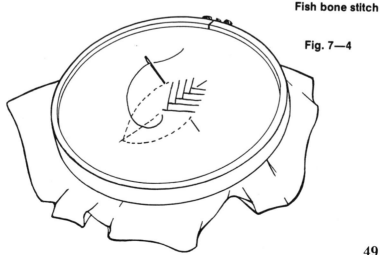

8. COUCHING STITCHES

Couching is a technique by which long threads are fastened down to the cloth with shorter stitches. Couching provides well defined outlines for motifs, or fillings with a padded appearance when worked in rows. The base (or "laid" threads and or stitches) can be metallic or other threads that are difficult to work with—or too precious to waste on the wrong side of the fabric.

SIMPLE COUCHING STITCH

The simplest method of couching holds down a thread or threads with tiny, regular tacking stitches. In addition to working a single row for an outline, the trailing ends of the laid thread can be turned back to form a new row, tacked down, and turned again for solid filling.

To work a single line, bring the thread or threads to be laid to the front of the fabric. If the line is of a definite length, the ends of the laid thread can be brought down through to the back of the fabric, to be secured by the couching stitches. Otherwise, the ends can trail until the line is finished. Hold the laid threads down on the cloth with the right thumb. Bring up the tacking thread (which can be of a contrasting color or lighter weight if desired) to the front of the fabric a short distance from the left end of the laid thread. Take a tiny stitch over the laid thread and bring the needle out to the front of the fabric again a short distance to the right along the guideline (Fig. 8—1A). Continue tacking the laid thread at regular intervals, holding the laid threads firmly so that it does not bend or pucker (B). If you are working in rows, place the couching stitches in a pattern to improve the appearance of the work (C).

Simple couching stitch

Fig. 8—1A

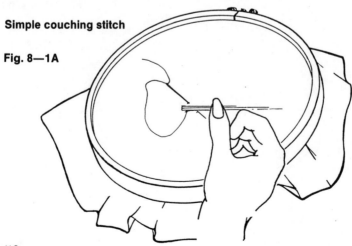

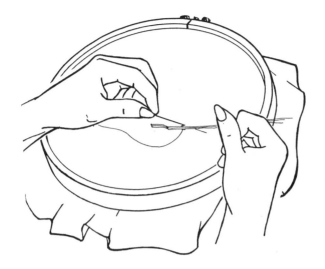

Fig. 8—1B

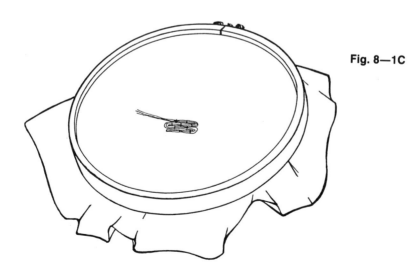

Fig. 8—1C

SATIN COUCHING STITCH

Many different kinds of stitches can be used to fasten down the laid thread. Among them are blanket stitches, cross stitches, ladder stitches, and simple groups of two or three closely placed tacking stitches. In all of these stitches, the laid thread is still an important part of the color and design. But in satin couching, the laid thread provides only a raised base for the overcast stitches. It is highly effective for scrolling tendril designs: hence its other name, the trailing stitch.

As in simple couching, bring the laid thread through to the front of the fabric and remove from the needle. Then, with the second thread, work closely spaced overcast stitches to secure the laid thread to the fabric (Figs. 8—2A and B).

Satin couching

Fig. 8—2A

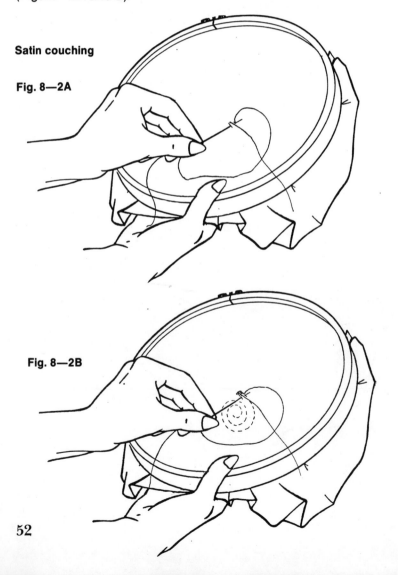

Fig. 8—2B

ROUMANIAN COUCHING

Also known as the oriental stitch, this is a self-couching stitch. That is, the same thread is used both for the laid thread and for the tacking stitches. It is useful as a solid filling stitch and is more economical of thread than the satin stitch.

Work from the bottom of the area to be covered. Bring the needle to the front of the fabric at the right guideline of the pattern area. Insert it at the left guideline and bring the needle through to the front again a little above the long stitch, about one-third of the way across the area (Fig. 8—3A). Pull the needle through. Insert the needle a little below the long stitch and a little to the right to cross it at a shallow diagonal angle. Bring the needle through to the front again on the right guideline slightly above the previous stitch, and pull it through (B). Continue in the same manner, working the stitches close together (C).

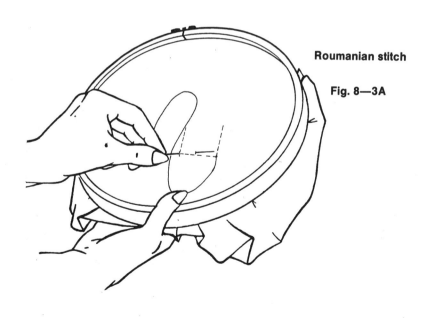

Roumanian stitch

Fig. 8—3A

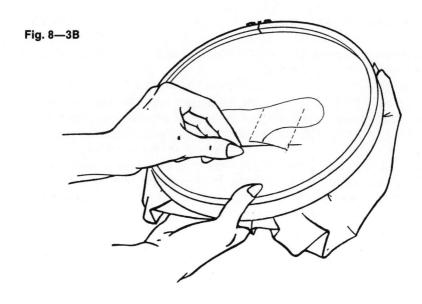

Fig. 8—3B

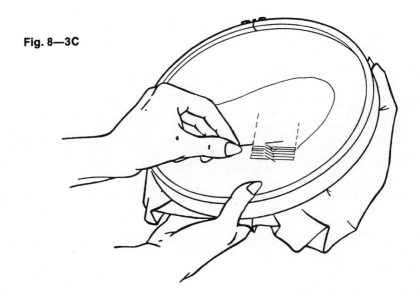

Fig. 8—3C

9. SATIN STITCHES

One of the loveliest and apparently simplest of filling stitches, the satin stitch is actually quite tricky. It takes practice to lay the stitches evenly and maintain an even edge. The stitches must not be too long, or they will not lie in the neat, lustrous rows that give this stitch its name. There are several techniques for breaking up the space to be filled so that the stitches are all of manageable length. If the direction of the stitch is changed from one area to another, it will create a pronounced difference in shade—a beautiful effect if that is what you want.

SATIN STITCH

The basic satin stitch is simply a series of straight stitches worked parallel to each other and close enough together to hide the fabric below (Figs. 9—1A and B). Take care to maintain an even tension. A lightly padded effect is created by first outlining the motif in split stitches—which will also assist in maintaining a regular outline.

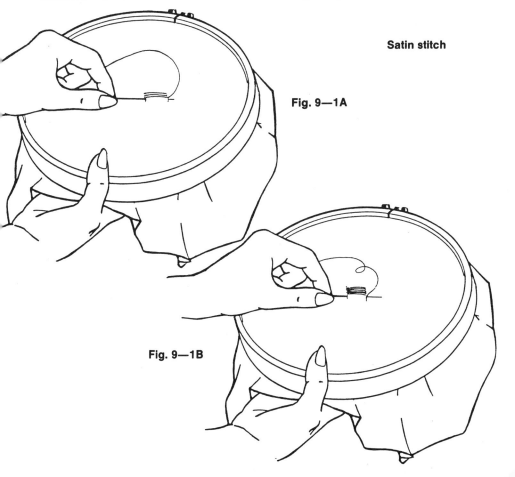

Satin stitch

Fig. 9—1A

Fig. 9—1B

ENCROACHING SATIN STITCH

This is one method of breaking up areas to be filled, and also provides a means of shading within a shape.

Divide the shape into parallel rows. The color of the thread may be darkened or lightened gradually from one row to the next. Work a row of basic satin stitches at the top of the motif. Work the second row of satin stitches so that the tops of the stitches lie between the bases of the two stitches in the row above (Fig. 9—2). The alternation in the position of the stitches gives a softer blending of the two rows.

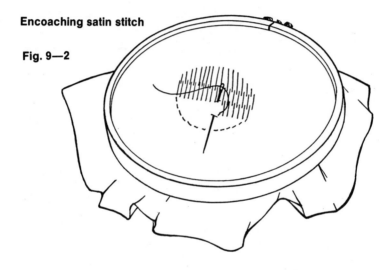

Encoaching satin stitch

Fig. 9—2

LONG-AND-SHORT STITCH

An even more subtle blending of shades and colors is possible with this stitch, which is named for the alternating stitches in the first row of work. This stitch is the easiest of the satin variations and the most amenable to irregular shapes.

Work in the same manner as for the basic satin stitch, except that long and short stitches alternate in the first row (Fig. 9—3A). On subsequent rows, work all stitches as long stitches, except when the end of the shape demands a shorter stitch (B). End with a row of short stitches.

Satin stitch, long and short

Fig. 9—3A

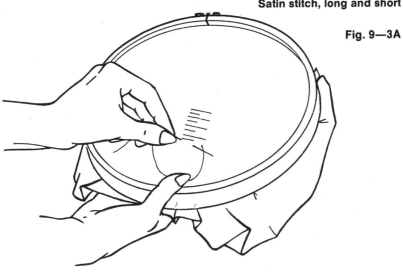

Fig. 9—3B

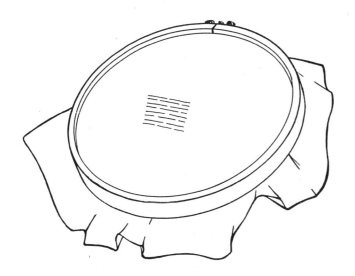

PADDED SATIN STITCH

Padding the satin stitch gives a motif a raised appearance. Padding works particularly well for leaves or flower shapes, for which the single layer of satin stitch may leave too jagged an edge of stitches at the pointed end.

Work one layer of satin stitches within the pattern area. Then turn the needle and the work and cover the first layer with another, closely worked layer of satin stitches at a different angle. To define the area even more crisply, work stem stitches, split stitches, or running stitches around the outline before working the first layer of satin stitches. When the work is completed, only the top satin stitches will be seen. (See Fig. 9—4.)

Padded satin stitch

Fig. 9—4

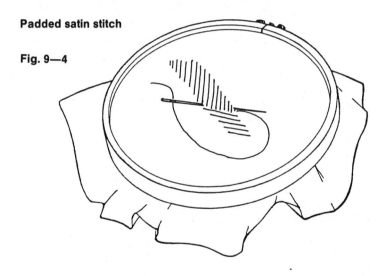

10. LAID FILLING STITCHES

These stitches are used to cover large pattern areas in needlework such as Jacobean embroidery. Because they essentially form grid designs, they are worked most easily on even-weave fabrics or those with a printed grid. These stitches are effective with two or more colors of thread, one for the basic lattice and the other for the tacking or ornamental stitches.

TRELLIS STITCH

This stitch works as well in a round or oblong shape as in one with squared corners. Simply work the long stitches to the edge of the desired curve. The trellis provides an airy but substantial-looking lattice design. To form the lattice, lay long, parallel straight stitches from one edge of the area to be covered to the other. Begin each new stitch on the same side of the pattern as the last stitch was completed so that threads do not cross underneath the fabric and possibly tangle or show through on the front. These stitches must be a uniform distance from one another. When the first row is completed, turn the work and lay the second row perpendicular to the first. These are the "laid" stitches. With another thread, of a second color if you wish, tack down each intersection with a small straight stitch. (See Fig. 10—1.) One variation of the trellis is the elongated trellis. This is one of the densest of filling stitches. Worked in one or two colors, it makes a very strong area of color with a regular, padded texture. Begin in the same fashion as for the trellis, taking straight stitches across the pattern at uniform intervals. When placing the perpendicular stitches, though, space them twice the distance apart. Anchor the intersections with tacking stitches; then use satin stitches to fill each rectangle.

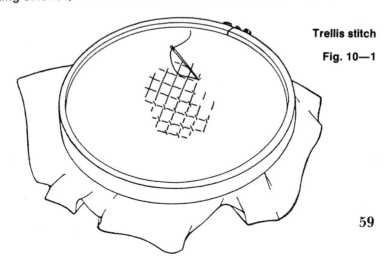

Trellis stitch

Fig. 10—1

INTERSECTED TRELLIS STITCH

This is a trellis variation with a denser appearance and a stronger second-color presence. After working the laid stitches of the trellis, work a small cross stitch over each intersection. In the center of each square, work a short, upright straight stitch. (See Fig. 10—2.) Similar to the intersected trellis (except that the laid stitches are worked in a diagonal pattern, rather than in a vertical and horizontal lines) is the French knot trellis. The change in the direction of the trellis is important when various laid filling stitches are located close together in the pattern. Work the laid stitches in diagonal rows. Using contrasting thread, tack each intersection with a tiny cross stitch and work a large French knot inside each diamond.

A further variation of the trellis is the stem stitch trellis. Because no tacking stitches are needed on this trellis, the lines of the lattice give the illusion of being straighter and more defined. Work stem stitches in diagonal rows, across the pattern in each direction. In contrasting thread, work an upright cross stitch in the center of each diamond.

Intersected trellis stitch

Fig. 10—2

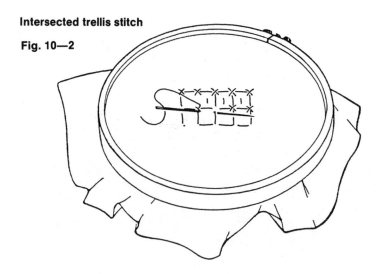

BACK- AND CROSS-STITCH

This stitch is not precisely a "laid" filling, but provides a similar result. The center cross stitches are frequently worked in a second color. Work squares of backstitch over the area to be filled. Be sure that each stitch covers the same number of threads. Work a cross stitch from corner to corner inside each square. (See Fig. 10—3.)

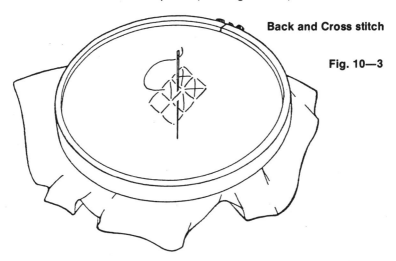

Back and Cross stitch

Fig. 10—3

BLOCK FILLING STITCH

With its denseness and texture and color contrasts, the block filling is one of the most dramatic of filling stitches. It usually looks best used in smaller areas. Fill the space with laid stitches worked fairly close together in one direction only. Using contrasting thread, tack the laid stitches down with blocks of satin stitch, arranged in a checkerboard pattern. (See Fig. 10—4.)

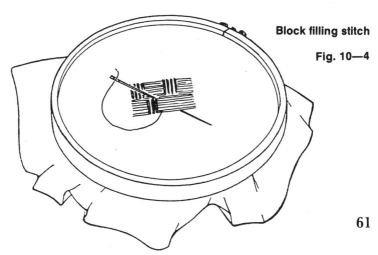

Block filling stitch

Fig. 10—4